The Forest:
An African Traditional Definition

Ekpe Inyang

Langaa Research & Publishing CIG
Mankon, Bamenda

Publisher:

Langaa RPCIG
Langaa Research & Publishing Common Initiative Group
P.O. Box 902 Mankon
Bamenda
North West Region
Cameroon
Langaagrp@gmail.com
www.langaa-rpcig.net

Distributed in and outside N. America by African Books Collective
orders@africanbookscollective.com
www.africanbookscollective.com

ISBN: 9956-792-46-2

Table of Contents

Preface

I strongly hold the view that for the seeds of conservation to germinate and grow into acceptable plants in Africa, they should be culturally quarantined, culturally sensitive, and anthropocentric in growth. The common dilemma facing conservationists on this continent is that the concepts and models that are used are imported from cultures that are strong advocates of strict eco-centric approach to conservation. Often a certain breed of conservationists adamantly refuses to buy the idea of an anthropocentric fine-tuning in some situations, and even fail to recognise the cushioning role that certain traditional beliefs and customs can play in the implantation of the foreign concepts and models into the host-cultures. The result has often been utter frustration on their part and hostile resentment on the part of the local people who unequivocally refuse to be partners in the conservation initiative.

The forest: an African traditional definition is aimed at providing the conservationist with some basic ideas as to which cultural areas to explore (using a few African cultures—from some ecologically and culturally rich forest zones of Cameroon that has earned the description of Africa in miniature due to its diversity and representativeness of ecological and cultural landscape that reflect the continent—for illustration) in order to direct him or her to the appropriate beliefs and customs that could be exploited in favour of conservation. There is no overemphasising that most, if not all, African cultures have at least some rudimentary aspects of conservation in the modern sense. These aspects constitute the strong colours that could be used to create an indelible picture of 'the importance of conservation' on the continent.

However, the task of translating the various cultural traditions, taboos, and customs within the context of modern conservation principles and practice is intentionally left in the hands of the conservationist. I do hope that this mere presentation of cultural artefacts would prove a meaningful exercise that could guide conservationists to assign an African definition to conservation in Africa. This, in my conviction, is the only way that can guarantee that all our efforts today will not simply be turned into an ugly heap of waste tomorrow.

Ekpe Inyang, 1998

1 _____

Culture-nature relationship

The forest subtly prompts a dialogue between culture and nature, the meaning and significance of which change with time and space. This dialogue constitutes the culture-nature relationship determined by our systems of belief, concepts, perceptions, values and attitudes that influence our treatment and use of natural resources.

These resources mean different things to different people, depending on the aspect of the culture—traditional, religious, scientific, technological, social, political or economic—that is the dominant influence. This is so because each of these cultural domains interacts with nature in a variety of different ways at various times and in different situations, thus presenting diverse threats, opportunities and experiences for various people.

Sacred forests and nature conservation

In most, if not all rural forest communities in Cameroon and Nigeria (and this may be true also for most of rural Africa), the forest is regarded as home of the ancestors, some of whom are in the form of the great creatures that dwell in it. It is also regarded as the abode of the spirits of the land, including malevolent and benevolent spirits, and a repository of some faith. In this regard, some forest areas are set aside and designated as sacred, forbidding therein the execution of such disturbing human activities as hunting, trapping, and farming. It is held that the destruction of a sacred forest could provoke the occurrence of a windstorm or natural calamities of the like, including epidemics of some dangerous diseases like small pox.

How a particular forest gains recognition as a sacred place is linked to some supernatural experiences by those believed to have 'four eyes', such as witches and wizards. 'Four-eyed' individuals also include herbalists, seers, fortune-tellers, visionaries and traditional priests who are believed to have the supernatural powers and abilities to see beyond the ordinary world, and can communicate effectively with and tap a lot of knowledge from Nature. They often show profound respect in their exploitation and utilization of natural resources, and have naturally developed the habit of planting and taking care of herbs, especially those with some medicinal values or magical powers. Their close contact and spiritual communication with Nature have given them the rare opportunity not only to experience Nature in that special way but also to be able to interpret some aspects of the natural world, hence their ability to identify sacred forest areas.

Some aspects of the physical environment, for example the preponderance of certain tree species associated with power or divinity, or even the very nature of the landscape, provide distinct features that distinguish sacred forests. A landscape dressed in a wonderful splendour of magical beauty—decorated with fascinating features like boulders, caves and lakes, for instance—or endowed with uncommon plant and animal species, is said to belong to the ancestors. A typical example of a sacred forest is the core area of Mount Kupe of the Bakossi village of Nyasoso in southwest Cameroon, where an alluring number of plant and animal species enjoys this rare cultural protection. This forest, which is considered as 'home of the ancestors', also provides a good watershed for Nyasoso and the environs. It is believed that the power that gives life to the whole of Bakossi ethnic group dwells in this mountain which, in turn, receives power from the forest. Of course, this belief also gains validity and credibility in ecological terms. The forest is habitat or, in this context text, repository of not only animals but also supernatural beings.

It is important to note that the above category of the sacred forest, "the ancestor's home", is large in size, compared to the next category we shall consider below. It may not have distinctly marked boundaries, but villagers traditionally grow up to appreciate and recognise its extent, and there is hardly a history of encroachment into it. The very belief in the attendant result should there be any encroachment—serious illness or even death—is enough deterrent.

The next category of the sacred forest is associated with traditional cults. Traditional cults or secret societies form an integral part of most rural African communities and traditions, some of which enjoy the singular privilege of owning special forests designated after their names and similarly considered as sacred. Cultic sacred forests are generally much smaller in size but much more defined than those normally associated with the ancestors. They usually have traditional signs to indicate their locations in order to warn non-members from trespassing. These are conspicuously displayed at the main entrances. It should be noted that even members themselves are restricted from entering the forest without good reasons for doing so. The clear occasions when members are allowed in are during traditional rituals and ceremonies.

A good example of a cultic sacred forest is the Ekpe (also called Nyamkpe) forest, common in most of Manyu and Ndian village communities in southwest Cameroon and some ethnic groups, such as Ejagham and Okoyong, in the Cross River State of Nigeria. Ekpe, which literally means the 'Leopard', is the highest traditional society or institution in these cultural areas. The name itself symbolizes power and authority, the leopard believed to be the most powerful animal in the forest. This shows the relationship between the human community and the animal community. As a symbol of this important relationship, every traditionally conscious community erects a special hall named after the institution (society). In the front of the hall are, usually, paintings of a leopard and other animals of cultural significance. There may be paintings depicting other aspects of the culture, such as the principal occupations of the people. The hall itself contains an enormous collection of haphazardly displayed exhibits of historical and cultural importance.

In the Korup ethnic group, two species of symbolic trees are planted in front of the hall. This seems to serve as a reminder to the fact that the society owes its power to the forest, which also gives it that unique identity. One of the species has been observed to naturally attract weaver birds which build their nests on the branches. The weaver birds are believed to influence the growth in the population of the villages, hence it is forbidden to kill, let alone eat, this species of birds.

Traditional societies and the forest

Any given culture is greatly influenced by the natural environment against whose background it is set. The environment provides the solid base for the necessary experiences that give rise to the basic cultural expressions. It also provides the colour and flavour that combine to define what is popularly referred to as cultural identity. All this can, however, be modified or adulterated by long periods of interactions with related or unrelated cultures.

The life and power of the traditional societies of the African forest ethnic groups lie in the forest. This gains credence not only from the mere fact that some of these societies have 'forest-homes' where all rites and ceremonies are performed, but more so because the elements that give them power are gotten from the forest.

Some of the societies have masquerades whose very outfits are made of materials obtained from the forest. For example, the outfit of the Ekpe masquerade is made from raffia palm and other special forest fibres. Also, as part of its outfit, the masquerade handles a leafy tree branch in the right hand, and uses this to pay obeisance to titled men or men of some respectable status, including those who may not necessarily be of the same culture, such as senior (government) officers.

It is also important to note that the Ekpe symbol is a leafy tree branch forced into a split stick pinned in the ground. This is used to warn against encroachment into an occupied or disputed forest plot, or an area that deserves some kind of protection, for example that which is adjacent to the source of water supply. It is also used to mark off an area in the village, during ceremonies, where non-initiates must not approach. Anyone who violates this unspoken injunction is sure to face a severe penalty, which is usually a very heavy fine.

The use of a leafy tree branch as the Ekpe symbol, or the very fact that the outfits of most traditional masquerades are made of materials obtained from the forest, helps to reinforce the relationship between the forest and some cultures, in some ways. It also points to the dependence of some cultures on the forest. Put the other way round, as we have already noted, some cultures also help to give some form of protection to the forest.

Community life and totemism

There is a multiplicity of traditional legends and folk tales in some cultures that point to the intricate relationship between humans and the so-called lesser creatures. The common belief is that there are some supernatural forces that control all living forms and that there are some lesser creatures that exist as the totems of some ethnic groups, clans or individuals. This is known in anthropomorphic terms as totemism, which includes the sacredness of some creatures as well as the ability of some individuals to transform into lesser creatures and live what could be described as 'double existence'. This means that such a human being has a representation of himself or herself in a completely animal form that dwells in the natural habitat.

Although the human representation, aptly referred to as totem, lives with and like other animals of its kind, it seems to be influenced, behaviourally and intellectually, by the human-host. This should not, however, drive us to hope to find an animal with the intelligence or behaviour of a human—the animal traits predominate. What is important to note is that the totem is far cleverer than the ordinary animal, and can perform some tasks or activities in accordance with the desire and plan of the *human-host*. For example, a human whose totem is a crocodile may decide to rescue a drowning man or just kill him. It is not strange to hear that a crocodile has killed someone; but there are also instances where crocodiles have saved drowning men by pushing them carefully ashore. There were occasions in the history of Korup when some young men were swept away by the main river of the ethnic group, and were later discovered lying unconscious on a bank up-river. Traditionally, such victims are not allowed to disclose what they saw, but it is generally held that totem-crocodiles are responsible for lending rescuing hands in such situations.

Humans who have elephants as their totems are known to organise themselves into groups and move about from village to village, raiding farms. The common belief in the Korup, Banyangi, Bakossi and Bakweri ethnic groups, to name but a few, is that members of one village may belong to an elephant cult that includes members of one or more other villages. The general rule is that every member must take the group to his or her own village and leads them to the farms that are condemned to face destruction. It is said that members' farms are hardly destroyed, and that, most often, the targets are the most progressive farmers in the village.

Originally, the essence of people transforming into animals or owning totems was connected with personal security, super-natural powers and prestige. When I was a child, an uncle, who was then very old, used to tell us stories about some great men of Korup. One of the popular stories was that of a hunter who quickly transformed into a leopard when he was attacked by a group of chimps after shooting at one of them. When the chimps saw the leopard, they fled for their dear lives, and that was how the hunter was saved.

There is that inseparable bond between the totem and the human-host, so much so that what affects one affects the other. There are stories of men and women who have lost their lives as a result of the fact that their totems have been killed by hunters. Unfortunately, animals that are commonly used as totems—elephant, buffalo, chimpanzee, gorilla, leopard, crocodile, python and bush pig—are easy prey to hunters.

10

It is important to note that habitat destruction contributes even more to the rapid extermination of animal species, including the totems. Recognizing this, some African cultures have used various methods to protect some forest areas or water bodies, basically to safeguard the lives, especially, of totems that belong to an entire human community. A case in point is the Asu Hill forest at Nguti in southwest Cameroon where a group of chimpanzees, which were considered as totems, enjoyed a considerably quiet and undisturbed environment.

The Asu Hill is also associated with Miankum (or Esapa), a powerful cult of the Mbo, Bakossi and Bassossi peoples. This important association helps to instil fear in the inhabitants and, therefore, ensures the full protection of the hill forest. The general belief is that any unauthorized entry into the forest, especially for an illegal activity such as hunting, can provoke the wrath of Miankum. Miankum abhors noise, and disturbing its home, such as the Asu Hill, would invariably result in the permanent incapacitation if not downright disappearance of the offender.

Another case in point is Deket d'Ekwe in Korup. Deket d'Ekwe, which literally means Pool of the Leopard, is believed to be home also of the tribal totem. This totem, a python, is believed to be responsible for the fish resources of the entire ethnic group. Its magical smell is believed to attract fish, which it leads to good and safe spawning areas. In the good old days, no one neared this pool for fishing or, even, swimming. It was believed that either the leopard would tear you up or the python would strangle and swallow you.

The significance of taboos and customs

Taboos and customs form a significant part of the African belief and value systems. These were and, in some cultures that are yet to be greatly influenced by Western thinking and concepts, are fundamental to some African lifestyles.

In Korup, as in most of the neighbouring cultures, there is a strong belief in the existence of what is popularly known as the 'King Tree'. This tree is said to stand apart from the rest of the trees in the forest, and is associated with something mystical. It is held that it has the ability to disappear from place to place, in reaction to changes in the environment. It is a powerful medicinal tree that cannot be harvested by an ordinary person. Stories have it that any creature that comes in contact with it dies immediately. It is in this regard that even powerful herbalists must perform a ceremony before approaching it. The ceremony consists of the sacrifice of a white cock, to determine whether or not it is safe to go near and harvest the needed parts.

There are also a good number of other trees that are associated with something supernatural. These include tree species that have been invaded by spirits. These spirits use such trees as their homes or hideouts. Stories abound as to how this category of trees manifests themselves. Some stories have it that on trying to fell such trees, pure blood may ooze out as a warning. Some trees are said to have stood up, erect, after they had been cut down. Other stories say that at certain hours of the day you could hear human voices that seem to come from within such trees. Persistent attempts at felling any of such trees are believed to result in the instant death of the feller.

As has been noted earlier on, sacred forests also occupy an important place in some African cultures. As the name implies, they are forest territories that are accorded some reverence or respect. They represent either the homes of the ancestors and gods of the land or of the spirits of some traditional cults and societies. They also represent places of worship where traditional ceremonies and rituals are performed. No other form of human activity is allowed in or near them, as the slightest disturbance could bring misfortune on the offender.

In some cultures, it is forbidden to kill a python and a 'two-headed' snake. These are sacred snakes that deserve special treatment. In the culture of the Ibo people in Nigeria, the python is considered as the representative of the ancestors and gods of the land. This snake must not be hurt even if it was found in your bed.

In Korup and most neighbouring ethnic groups, the 'two headed' snake, which symbolizes twins, receives the same treatment. Additionally, if a woman came across this snake she immediately looked for powder or chalk (if either could be found around) and sprinkled this on its body in the same way as a mother would on her baby. Also, particular kind of beautiful caterpillars, which are supposedly rare, are treated with care. It is believed that if a woman who is known to be barren encounters this type of caterpillar, it symbolises that she has a promise of childbirth. Such a woman (if she were brave enough) would pick up the sacred creature and touched her nipples with it as a way of saying, "May it be so!"

Again, in the Korup ethnic group, there are some animals that are not supposed to be eaten by females. These include all species of the cat family, the yellow-backed duiker and the python. Any female who breaks this custom, it is believed, can become infertile. Also, it is forbidden for pregnant women to eat animals such as bush pigs, for the simple fear that doing so could produce deformed children.

In most rural cultures, the python cannot be killed and eaten without, at least, presenting the bile to the village head. This is closely linked to the common fear that its bile could be used by some individuals to poison their enemies. Similarly, in the Korup ethnic group, a leopard, which is considered as 'meat-for-the-village' (although eaten only by males), is considered not to belong to an individual or a family alone. Even if already butchered, the village head has the responsibility of asking for the bile and whiskers. This is also associated with the fear that these parts, which are also regarded as poisonous, could be used to commit atrocities in the village or the ethnic group at large.

In most African cultures, the owl is associated with witchcraft. Its visage and hooting sound, coupled with its nocturnal lifestyle, seems to create some kind of aura around it. There is a general belief in the Korup ethnic group that killing this bird, except inadvertently, could bring one untold misfortune. The worst one can do to this fearsome bird, if one is 'honestly' frightened by its hooting, is to loudly curse and wish it hell and then walk off instantly.

Inspiration streaming from Nature

A lone and communicative walk in the forest normally generates a feeling of awe and wonder in some people; in many others, it instils fear. In my world of imagination, the forest represents a puzzling ocean of magnitude, a body that constantly emits some form of cosmic energy and which contains an enormous store of information. It should not come as a surprise for you to see some people, such as herbalists and fortune-tellers, occasionally taking meditative walks in the forest. This is essentially for them to gain some knowledge and power. To paraphrase and add to the words of Walter Russell in his introduction to Lao Russell's philosophical book entitled *Love*, anyone who is in constant (spiritual) dialogue with Nature is enabled to gain knowledge cosmically; that is, from the natural world. This form of knowledge, I would suppose, increases one's intellectual capabilities and potentialities and, perhaps, places one at a level that is far above that of an average person.

The artistic expression of any given clan or ethnic group is greatly influenced by the culture itself which, as we have already noted, is influenced by the natural environment. This presupposes that any culture owes a significant part of its identity to the natural environment. A cursory look at the paintings and carvings of most African forest ethnic groups testifies to the reflections of these art forms of myths and folk tales related to the forest.

It is of great importance also to take a critical look at some African religion, music, and nomenclature. These are areas where you find a lot drawn from the natural environment. The forest provides a generous source of inspiration, especially for those who truly and genuinely appreciate its value and power of magic.

The forest as community property

It is generally claimed by most rural African communities that the forest is a free gift from God (Nature) or a legacy handed down from generation to generation by the ancestors. It is considered as the *bona fide* property of any given clan or ethnic group, and that only members of these cultural entities have the traditional or legitimate right of utilization or exploitation of its resources.

In some ethnic groups, such as Korup, Bakossi, Bassossi and Mbo, selling or pawning a piece of land is considered as gross violation and abuse of Nature, and this act is believed to be punishable under the judicial dispensation of the ancestors and land gods. However, the custom may allow a non-indigene to cultivate a piece of land or exploit a specified section of the forest upon the procurement of a few items for traditional libation. This is done to obtain permission from the ancestors who enjoy the singular rights and prerogatives to allow any non-indigene to use any tribal piece of land under certain conditions. The piece of land, excluding all that is grown on it, remains the property of the ethnic group. In fact, the land, and in some cases whatever grows on it, reverts to the ethnic group upon the death or departure of the non-indigene. However, in a situation where the non- indigene married from the ethnic group, the land is automatically inherited by his wife and their offspring, if any.

When a piece of land becomes the sole property of an individual or a family, it is up to that individual or family to decide on how best to manage it. The custom does not forbid or restrict the sale of this category of land and, at the same time, does not encourage it. The common policy is for the next generation of family members to be given the opportunity also of enjoying the family property.

In the Bakossi ethnic group, the forest outside areas designated as sacred, which, according to the people, does not belong to the government (protected area) and which lies within a few kilometres of the village is divided amongst (extended) families who act as the immediate custodians. This means that when a child is born in a village, he or she can cultivate only in the forest area that belongs to his or her extended family.

This is in sharp contrast with the Korup ethnic group which holds that the forest remains the common property of the village community in particular and ethnic group as a whole, so long as it is still in its natural or virgin state. This presupposes that a piece of the forest can only become the property of an individual or family if and when it has undergone total transformation through effective agricultural intervention. It means that ownership cannot and does not result from mere forest demarcation.

But there is this customary arrangement which provides that the forest in front of a farm plot, up to a distance that is not quite defined, is under the custodianship of the owner of that plot. No other person, for whatever reason, is permitted to cultivate in that area, except with the expressed permission of the traditionally recognised custodian. This seems to be a way of avoiding land disputes as individuals are encouraged to stick to a particular forest territory. What would normally push one out of one forest area into another is when the soil fails to respond to the effort and if the area is prone to invasion by marauding animals or some other calamity.

In the Korup mythology, the forest is regarded as the healing station of life. This seems to emanate from the fact that traditional or folk medicine, which has been so effective and so popular in the ethnic group, depends chiefly on what the forest offers.

Traditional medicine as a natural gift

Traditional medicine is an important ingredient of the cultures of most rural communities in Africa. A good knowledge of medicinal plants adds to one's status and respect in the society. In some ethnic groups, such as Korup, a child is exposed to the use of medicinal plants to treat minor cuts and petty ailments like stomach upsets, coughs and minor skin diseases, as early as the age of seven.

In the Korup ethnic group, there are some cures that are the exclusive monopoly of certain families. This monopoly of knowledge emanates from the belief in some special gift from the ancestors that is not transferrable. Any transfer of such a gift, be it to the closest friend, is believed to bring one some misfortune or curse. Such gifts include the ability to treat serious cases like cardiac problems and complicated fractures.

From time immemorial, rural communities in Africa have depended on traditional medicine for health. Some diseases are believed to be curable only with traditional medicines. There are some instances where people have been referred to traditional doctors when medical doctors realize that their cases are difficult to handle using orthodox medicine.

Traditional medicine, at a certain level, goes beyond the mere knowledge of and ability to concoct medicines using plants. There is also the application of supernatural elements and skills. This becomes necessary when cases are serious and are believed to be associated with witchcraft, charm or supernatural poisoning. In such situations, the herbalist or traditional doctor communicates with the gods and spirits of the land, through rituals which include offering some sacrifice to these supernatural beings. Sometimes, herbal or other forms of concoctions are smeared all over the body of the patient.

Most experienced herbalists harvest certain medicines in the evening, after the sun has gone to bed. The choice of this period is linked to the general belief that this is when the ancestral spirits and gods of the land, from whom most herbalists receive healing powers, come out. It is believed that these supernatural beings guide and direct the herbalists in the process of harvesting the plants and concocting the medicines. They also recommend the quantity to give to a patient and time the patient must receive treatment.

Some herbalists domesticate certain medicinal plants, which are planted around their compounds. Some of the plants are believed to keep away witches and wizards who might want to come around and test the powers of the herbalists. You may come across a herbalist walking around his compound, in powerful incantations, communicating with the plants in his magic garden. This is one of the moments that the herbalist might have suspected an evil attempt on his practice.

It might mean that some of the most potent plants he has been using to treat certain illnesses are no longer producing the intended results. His belief at this point could have been that some witch or wizard might have planted something evil in his compound, which has succeeded in reducing the efficacy of the medicinal plants he brings home. His purpose of communicating with his magical plants, therefore, might be to command them to fortify their guard against the evildoers.